WITHDRAWN

Exploring World Cultures

Cambodia

By Raymie Davis

Cavendish
Square
New York

Published in 2022 by Cavendish Square Publishing, LLC
29 East 21st Street New York, NY 10010

Copyright © 2022 by Cavendish Square Publishing, LLC

First Edition

No part of this publication may be reproduced, stored in a retrieval system, or transmitted in any form or by any means—electronic, mechanical, photocopying, recording, or otherwise—without the prior permission of the copyright owner. Request for permission should be addressed to Permissions, Cavendish Square Publishing, 29 East 21st Street New York, NY 10010. Tel (877) 980-4450; fax (877) 980-4454.

Website: cavendishsq.com

This publication represents the opinions and views of the author based on his or her personal experience, knowledge, and research. The information in this book serves as a general guide only. The author and publisher have used their best efforts in preparing this book and disclaim liability rising directly or indirectly from the use and application of this book.

All websites were available and accurate when this book was sent to press.

Library of Congress Cataloging-in-Publication Data

Names: Davis, Raymie, author.
Title: Cambodia / Raymie Davis.
Description: New York : Cavendish Square Publishing, [2022] | Series: Exploring world cultures | Includes bibliographical references and index.
Identifiers: LCCN 2020039594 | ISBN 9781502662439 (library binding) | ISBN 9781502662415 (paperback) | ISBN 9781502662422 (set) | ISBN 9781502662446 (ebook)
Subjects: LCSH: Cambodia--Juvenile literature.
Classification: LCC DS554.3 .D37 2022 | DDC 959.6--dc23
LC record available at https://lccn.loc.gov/2020039594

Editor: Caitie McAneney
Copyeditor: Jill Keppeler
Designer: Rachel Rising

The photographs in this book are used by permission and through the courtesy of: Cover, pp. 19, 23 hadynyah/E+/Getty Images; p. 4 Pakawat Thongcharoen/Moment/Getty Images; p. 5 John D. Buffington/DigitalVision/Getty Images; p. 6 Narathip Ruksa/Moment/Getty Images; p. 7 GarySandyWales/E+/Getty Images; pp. 8, 11, 25 TANG CHHIN SOTHY/Contributor/AFP/Getty Images; pp. 9, 17 Matteo Colombo/Moment/Getty Images; p. 10 AFP/Stringer/AFP/Getty Images; p. 12 Thierry Falise/ Contributor/LightRocket/Getty Images; p. 13 Sumith Nunkham/Moment/Getty Images; p. 14 Todd Brown/Stone/Getty Images; p. 15 TANG CHHIN SOTHY/Stringer/AFP/Getty Images; p. 16 Graham Lucas Commons/Stockbyte/Getty Images; p. 18 Kriangkrai Thitimakorn/Moment/Getty Images; p. 20 saiko3p/Shutterstock.com; p. 21 Martin Puddy/Stone/Getty Images; p. 22 Godong/Contributor/Universal Images Group/Getty Images; p. 24 Jack Vartoogian/Getty Images/Contributor/Archive Photos/Getty Images; p. 26 wichan sumalee/Moment/Getty Images; p. 27 Loop Images/Contributor/Universal Images Group/Getty Images; p. 28 Malcolm P Chapman/Moment/Getty Images; p. 29 cuongvnd/Moment/Getty Images.

Some of the images in this book illustrate individuals who are models. The depictions do not imply actual situations or events.

CPSIA compliance information: Batch #CW22CSQ: For further information contact Cavendish Square Publishing LLC, New York, New York, at 1-877-980-4450.

Printed in the United States of America

Find us on

Contents

Cambodia is home to old ruins, floating villages, and the Mekong River. It has grand temples called pagodas. It's also home to people with a rich history

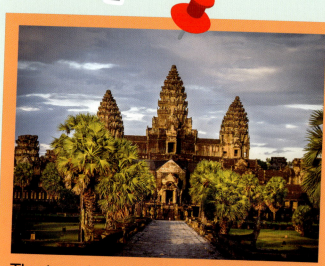

The temples of Angkor Wat were first Hindu, then Buddhist. They're at the center of the Cambodian flag.

and culture, or way of life.

Cambodia is located in Southeast Asia, on a **peninsula** that's sometimes called Indochina. Indochina also includes Vietnam, Laos, Thailand, Myanmar, and part of Malaysia. China and India heavily shaped the culture in this region, or part

of the world.
For much of
its history,
Cambodia was
on important
trade routes
between China,
India, and other
Southeast Asian

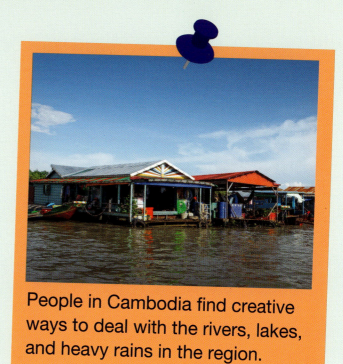

People in Cambodia find creative ways to deal with the rivers, lakes, and heavy rains in the region.

countries. Because of that, it's been a crossroads for cultural sharing between those regions.

Cambodia's culture is also greatly **influenced** by the belief systems of Buddhism and Hinduism. Their effects on Cambodia can be seen in the grand temples of the ancient city of Angkor.

Cambodia is only about 360 miles (579 kilometers) from east to west. It borders Thailand, Vietnam, and Laos. The Gulf of Thailand is to the southwest.

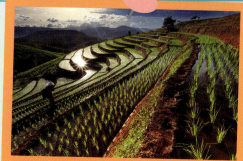

The central plain of Cambodia has grasslands and rice paddies, or wet land where rice is grown.

Cambodia's land is mostly plains. However, it does have mountains and forests. The Dangrek (Dângrêk) mountain range is found on Cambodia's border with Thailand. The Cardamom (Krâvanh) mountain range is in the west. The tallest mountain

FACT!

The word for mountain is "phnom" in Khmer, the language of Cambodia.

Cambodia has a tropical, or warm and wet, climate. The temperature in Cambodia is often more than 80 degrees Fahrenheit (26 degrees Celsius).

peak in Cambodia is Phnom Aural.

The Mekong River is the largest river in Southeast Asia. Starting in China, the Mekong

Asian elephants and several species, or kinds, of monkeys live in the forests of Cambodia.

cuts through Laos, Cambodia, and Vietnam. Then, it drains into the South China Sea. The Sab River connects the Mekong to Tonle Sap (Great Lake) in Cambodia. **Monsoon** season brings heavy rains to Cambodia, increasing the area of Tonle Sap. People live in fishing villages on this lake.

Ancient civilizations in Cambodia were influenced by ancient India and China. The Khmer Empire was the greatest ancient civilization in Cambodia. It built many of the ancient temples and other buildings Cambodia is known for. Much of Southeast Asia was under Khmer rule from the 9th century to the 13th century.

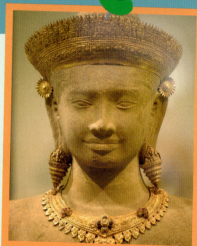

This ancient Cambodian jewelry is from the Angkor era—the time in which Angkor Wat was built.

The Khmer Empire later lost land to Vietnamese and Thai peoples. In 1863, Cambodia

FACT!

The temples of Angkor Wat were built around the 12th century.

asked for help from France. France then combined Vietnam, Laos, and Cambodia into the colony of French Indochina. Then, in 1953, Cambodia became independent.

Most Cambodians **converted** from Hinduism to Buddhism in the 13th century.

Cambodia suffered during the Vietnam War in the 1960s and 1970s. A **communist** group called the Khmer Rouge took control of Cambodia in 1975. The Khmer Rouge wiped out large parts of Cambodian culture in a four-year **genocide**.

Khmer Rouge

Pol Pot was the **dictator** of the Khmer Rouge. His orders led to the deaths of more than 2 million Cambodians. Many people were killed, while others died from overwork, sickness, and hunger.

VOTE ✓

Today, Cambodia is officially a kingdom. Its government is a constitutional monarchy with elements, or parts,

The military of Cambodia is called the Royal Cambodian Armed Forces (RCAF).

of a democracy. In a democracy, people have the ability to take part in government.

Cambodia's government has three branches. The legislative branch— or parliament—makes laws. It is made up of the Senate and National Assembly. The judicial branch is made up of courts

FACT!

A constitutional monarchy is led by a king or queen whose power is limited by a constitution.

Cambodia was a dictatorship in the past. Today, it still struggles with democracy. The government's actions are often unchecked. People can be harmed for speaking against it.

that are meant to protect the rights of citizens. The executive branch, which includes the king and prime minister, carries out laws. The prime minister is the head of government, while the king is the head of the armed

The Cambodian parliament meets in the capital city of Phnom Penh.

forces. The National Assembly votes for the prime minister, while the king's power is handed down through the royal family. The constitution, adopted in 1993, is meant to uphold fairness and justice in the country.

11

For much of Cambodia's history, people practiced subsistence farming. That means people farmed for food just for their family or community. People

Cambodia is one of the main producers of cassava, a root vegetable often eaten in Asia.

fished and grew rice, fruits, and vegetables. Until 1975, the national economy—its system of making, buying, and selling goods and services—depended on rice and rubber. The country would export, or sell, these goods to other countries. Unfortunately, the country's economy has suffered

FACT!

Cambodia is one of Asia's poorest countries.

Angkor **Archaeological** Park had 2.2 million visitors in 2019. The site made around $99 million. Many tourists come from the United States, South Korea, and China.

Traditional fishing tools in Southeast Asia include nets and baskets.

because of war, **poverty**, and bad weather.

Today, Cambodia makes money from tourism, or the business of travel. Cambodians work in hotels and restaurants that serve travelers. People still fish to get food for their families and to sell at markets. Rice is a major export. Farmers also grow sugarcane, soybeans, coconuts, and cassava. Cambodian factories manufacture, or make, clothes and shoes to export.

Like many Southeast Asian countries, Cambodia deals with monsoons. Strong winds bring heavy rains from May to October. Rainfall helps plants

Flooding in Cambodia is likely to increase due to **climate change**.

grow and provides water for native animals. Many animals and plants live in Cambodia because of its rich environment, or natural surroundings.

Cambodia also has environmental challenges. Heavy rains can lead to harmful flooding. Seasons that used to be expected and regular can be more

FACT!

Cambodia is home to 2,300 plant species.

Dealing with Water

Cambodia has a long history of overcoming water challenges. Ancient Angkor had systems to manage water, such as canals and long walls called dikes.

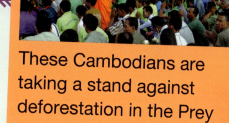

These Cambodians are taking a stand against deforestation in the Prey Lang Forest.

extreme because of climate change. Climate change also causes sea levels to rise, which is a problem in coastal regions. Flooding can lead to erosion, or the wearing down of soil.

Cambodia's natural environment has suffered due to human actions. People cut down too many trees, which is called deforestation. Poaching, or illegally hunting, animals like elephants has led to sharp decreases in wild animal populations.

15

More than 16.4 million people live in Cambodia. The population is increasing quickly. Most people in Cambodia have the same **ethnic** background—Khmer. The Khmer make

This Cham community lives along the banks of the Tonle Sap.

up about 97 percent of the total population of Cambodia. They live in the regions around the Tonle Sap and Mekong River, on the plains, and on the coast.

FACT!

Indigenous, or native, peoples mostly live in northeastern Cambodia. They include the Katu, Mnong, Jarai, and more.

Vietnamese in Cambodia

Many Vietnamese people had to flee Cambodia in the 1970s during the Khmer Rouge **regime.** Some of them moved back in the 1980s.

These Khmer women are in traditional dance dresses.

The second largest ethnic group is the Cham-Malay peoples. They make up less than 2 percent of Cambodia's population. In Cambodia, they are called the Khmer Islam or Western Cham. As Muslims, Cham communities tend not to mix much with the Khmer.

Smaller ethnic communities in Cambodia include Chinese, Vietnamese, Laotians, and some indigenous peoples. Indigenous people mostly live in highland areas away from others.

17

About 2 million people live in Phnom Penh, the largest city in Cambodia. Other cities include Battambang and Siem Reap. People get around cities on motorbikes and *tuk tuks*, which are a kind of passenger cart.

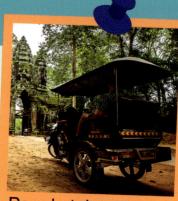

People take *tuk tuks* through the Cambodian city of Siem Reap.

However, most people in Cambodia live in rural, or country, villages. Traditional Cambodian houses are built on wooden pilings over water. The roofs are thatched, or made from dried plant

FACT!

Many Cambodians lost family members at the hands of the Khmer Rouge.

Women in Cambodia

Women in Cambodia had to take jobs in the 1970s when the Khmer Rouge killed many men. Women have equal rights in Cambodia today, but tradition holds them back from some jobs.

matter. People often farm or fish for a living. Sometimes children have to help with work.

Most families live in rural areas of Cambodia.

Families are very important in Cambodia. Parents and children live together until a child gets married and starts their own household. Children are taught to respect their elders and do chores to help the family. People under 15 make up the highest portion of the population in Cambodia.

About 95 percent of Cambodia's population is Theravada Buddhist. The goal of Buddhism is to reach enlightenment, which is a kind of spiritual awakening and an end to suffering.

The center of Buddhism in Cambodia is Wat Ounalom in Phnom Penh.

Buddhists follow the teachings of Siddhartha Gautama (Buddha). He lived in India and Nepal thousands of years ago. Siddhartha was a prince, but he left his kingdom once he became aware of human suffering. He came up with a way of

FACT!

Visak Bochea Day in Cambodia celebrates the birth of Siddhartha Gautama.

Other Religions

Other Cambodians may be Christians, Muslims, Jews, or Baha'is. Some practice indigenous religions, or those native to Cambodia.

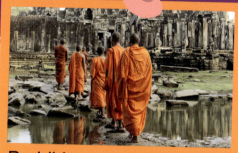

Buddhist monks wear orange robes.

living that could help people achieve enlightenment. He spread his teachings and gained followers—Buddhist monks. Buddhism then spread throughout East and Southeast Asia.

Buddhism shaped Cambodia. During the Khmer Rouge regime of the 1970s, religions, or organized belief systems, were outlawed in Cambodia. Many monks had to flee Cambodia. Today, Buddhism is the state religion of Cambodia, and many monks call Cambodia home.

Language

Most Cambodians speak the Khmer language. It is the official language of Cambodia. There are more than 18 million speakers, and it's also spoken

This schoolteacher is writing in Khmer.

by people in parts of Vietnam and Thailand. Some people in Cambodia also speak French, Vietnamese, and Chinese.

Khmer is a kind of Mon-Khmer language. This is a language family with about 130 languages. These languages, which include Vietnamese, are spoken in many countries in Southeast Asia.

FACT!

About 90 percent of Cambodians speak Khmer.

Different Dialects

Dialects are different types of a language spoken from place to place. Standard Khmer, spoken in central Cambodia, is a little different from Khmer spoken in other parts of Cambodia, Thailand, and Vietnam.

To say hello to your friends in Khmer, use *susadei* (pronounced soos-a-day).

Khmer has roots in Sanskrit and Pali languages, which were both widely used in ancient India. Many Hindu texts were written in Sanskrit. Many classic texts in Theravada Buddhism were written in Pali.

Some indigenous people in Cambodia speak tribal languages. The most important tribal language in Cambodia is Cham. About 150,000 people in Cambodia speak Cham.

Art forms in Cambodia are often a mix of traditional Khmer styles and international influences. Cambodian artwork often uses ancient ideas. Artists make pottery, paintings, and woven artwork. Many art forms tell ancient Cambodian stories or

Apsaras are traditional Cambodian dances. The Royal Ballet in Phnom Penh keeps apsara traditions alive.

show Buddhist images. Some contemporary, or modern, artists use art to deal with the pain of Cambodia's genocide. Dance, theater, and music are also important to Cambodian culture.

FACT!

Artists and performers were killed by the Khmer Rouge. Today, artists are rebuilding Cambodian arts.

Music in Cambodia

Cambodian musicians often still use traditional instruments. These include wind instruments such as wooden flutes and string instruments such as lutes.

Festivals and holidays in Cambodia celebrate the country's history, Buddhist influences, and nature. People visit their families and hometown pagodas

Cambodians take part in a dragon boat race during the Water Festival.

during Khmer New Year and Pchnum Ben. During the Water Festival (or Bonn Om Touk), the cities of Siem Reap and Phnom Penh host colorful dragon boat races and fireworks. The festival marks how the Tonle Sap River changes course each year.

Taking care of animals, family members, and household duties aren't just jobs for adults in Cambodia. Kids have to help out too. However,

Kids often find ways to make their chores, such as caring for animals, fun.

people sometimes make these tasks fun. They also fly kites, watch television, or play games. Karaoke (singing along to music) is another fun pastime for Cambodians.

FACT!

Martial arts include different sports or skills that came from traditional fighting styles, especially in East Asia.

Kites and Culture

Kites often stand for freedom. Like religion, arts, and sports, they were outlawed under the Khmer Rouge. Today, Cambodians celebrate the Khmer Kite Flying Festival each year.

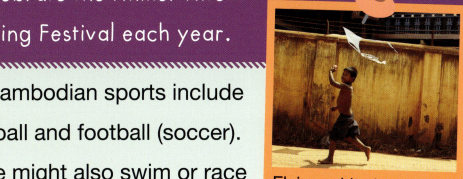
Flying a kite is a fun pastime for all ages.

Cambodian sports include volleyball and football (soccer). People might also swim or race canoes. One popular sport is Cambodian boxing. Cambodian boxing is a kind of martial art. Many East and Southeast Asian countries have their own martial arts traditions. Pradal Serey (also called Kun Khmer) is a Cambodian form of kickboxing. Bokator is a form of Khmer boxing, which uses unarmed skills as well as staffs and sticks.

The warm, wet environment of Cambodia affects what people eat there. Rice and fish are two major parts of the Cambodian diet. Rice grows widely in rice paddies in the plains of Cambodia. Fish are in great supply in Tonle Sap and the Mekong River.

Fried crickets, beetles, water bugs, and even spiders make a crunchy snack in Cambodia!

Large markets—indoor, outdoor, and even on the water—sell local fruits and vegetables. Native vegetables include Cambodian water spinach,

FACT!

Cattle, pigs, and buffalo are raised for food in Cambodia.

Cambodian soups include *kuy teav,* a noodle soup made with rice noodles and meat. *Samlor kako* is a spicy fish soup.

Thai basil, bean sprouts, and okra. Native fruits include tropical durians, passion fruit, dragon fruit, coconuts, and mangoes. Markets also sell seafood, from huge barbequed squid to crabs to grilled fish and shrimp.

This meal combines key Cambodian foods—rice, seafood, and tropical fruits.

Cambodian meals include rice bowls, noodle bowls, and soups. Pork and rice is a common breakfast. Enjoying Cambodian food is just one way to learn about this rich culture!

Glossary

archaeological   Having to do with the study of things that have been left behind by peoples of the past.

climate change   Change in Earth's weather caused by human activity.

communist   Referring to a way of organizing society where there is no privately owned property.

convert   To change from one thing into another.

dictator   Someone who runs a country by force.

ethnic   Of or relating to large groups of people who have the same cultural background and ways of life.

extreme   To a very great degree.

genocide   The systematic killing of a particular group or groups of people in a country.

influence   To have an effect on something.

monsoon   Seasonal winds that affect climate in the southern areas of Asia, resulting in wet spring and summer months and dry winter months.

peninsula   A piece of land that is connected to a mainland and is surrounded on three sides by water.

poverty   The state of being poor.

regime   A government in power.

traditional   Following what's been done for a long time.

Find Out More

Books

Klepeis, Alicia. *Cambodia*. Minnetonka, MN:
    Bellwether Media, 2019.
Mara, Wil. *Cambodia*. New York, NY: Children's
    Press, 2018.

Website
Angkor
www.nationalgeographic.com/travel/world-heritage/
angkor/
Explore Angkor Archaelogical Park with
National Geographic!

Video
**How Water Built and Destroyed This
Powerful Empire**
www.youtube.com/watch?v=yytrFWa-OH0
Learn about how geography and climate affected the
decline of Angkor.

Index

About the Author

Raymie Davis loves to learn about ancient ruins and cultural cuisine! She lives with two rescue animals and two humans.

31901067579229